100 WORDS

Kids Need to Read by 2nd Grade

Sight word practice to build strong readers

from the editors of Scholastic News

Scholastic
Professional Books

New York • Toronto • London • Auckland • Sydney

Contents

Dear Educator,

Teachers know and experts agree that the only way for children to master sight words—those high frequency, often non-decodable words essential to reading fluency—is through practice. With *100 Words Kids Need to Read,* we are pleased to offer a tool to help you provide that practice in an engaging, effective format.

We created the three books in this series—for first, second, and third graders—with the guidance of literacy experts and classroom teachers. Broken down into manageable groups, words are introduced in context and reinforced through inviting puzzles and games. Each sequence of activities is carefully designed to touch on reading, writing, and usage—taking children beyond mere visual recognition of sight words to genuine mastery.

The journey through these skill-building pages will help young readers make the successful transition from learning to read to reading to learn. Along the way, they will also receive excellent preparation for standardized tests. Enjoy the trip!

David Goddy

David Goddy
VP, Publisher

ANSWER KEY Page 4: 1. take; 2. his; him; 3. man; men; 4. all; none; *Sells smells* **Page 5:** 2. drink; 3. some; 4. slept; 5. sleep; 6. drank **Page 6:** 1. My father makes milkshakes all the time. 2. I think his milkshakes are the best. 3. Last week I drank a milkshake every day. 4. Today, Dad made some milkshakes. 5. Then he took a short nap. 6. While he slept, I drank a milkshake. 7. In fact, I drank them all. 8. I had a stomachache all day! **Page 7:** 2. brown; 3. white; 4. pretty, purple; 5. funny, short **Page 8:** 2. brother; 3. said; 4. read; 5. sister; 6. children; 7. ask; 8. say *Verbs:* read, said, say, took; *Nouns:* brother, school, children, sister; *Adjectives:* pretty, purple, funny, brown, short, white **Page 10:** From top, pictures match sentences 2, 3, 5, 4, 1 **Page 11:** 2. myself; 3. but; 4. make; 5. your; 6. our; 7. us **Page 12:** 2. r; 3. o; 4. b; 5. i; 6. n; *To get a robin* **Page 13:** 1. b; 2. a; 3. a; 4. a; 5. c; 6. c **Page 14:** 2. Tuesday; 3. third; 4. second **Page 15:** Answers will vary **Page 16:** 1. Every; 2. Many; 3. few; 4. any; 5. better; 6. best; 7. them;

Page 17: 1. please; 2. hello; 3. town; 4. help; 5. Thank; Goodbye; *soggy doggy* **Page 18:** 1. Hello! May I please buy some apples? 2. We buy apples here every year. 3. Few apples taste as good as these. 4. I won't buy any green apples. 5. I like red apples better than green. 6. Many apples are ripe. 7. Thanks for the apples; a pineapple. **Page 19:** 2. open; 3. there; 4. now; 5. after, before; 6. then **Page 20:** 2. Who is that? 3. What is your last name? 4. Why did school close? 5. Where are the books? 6. How did the dog reach the cookies? **Page 21:** *Who?* children, men, us; *Where?* here, school, there; *When?* after, before, now, soon **Page 22:** 1. early; 2. over; 3. end; 4. story; 5. quiet; 6. fell; 7. wide; 8. into; 9. more **Page 23:** 1. fall; 2. winter; 3. spring; 4. summer **Page 24:** 1. The opposite of early is late. 2. Another word for quiet is silent. 3. Another word for story is tale. 4. The opposite of more is less. 5. The opposite of over is under. 6. Another word for over is above. 7. Another word for end is finish.

Editor: Kaaren Sorensen **Art Directors:** Deborah Dinger, Joan Michael, Vanessa Frazier, Beth Benzaquin **Editorial Consultants:** Wiley Blevins, Mary C. Rose, Sue Sxczepanski **Writers:** Laine Falk, Spencer Kayden, Jessica B. Levine **Copy Editors:** L.C. Israel, Bryan Brown • **Magazine Group**: VP, Publisher: David Goddy • VP, Editor in Chief: Rebecca Bondor • Associate Editorial Director: Alyse Sweeney • Design Director: Judith Christ-Lafond • Production Director: Barbara Schwartz • Executive Director of Photography: Steven Diamond • Publishing System Director: David Hendrickson • Manager, Digital Imaging Group: Marc Stern • Director of Library Service: Bert Schacter • Library Manager: Maggie Stevaralgia • VP, Marketing: Jocelyn Forman • **Scholastic Education**: President: Margery Mayer • Group VP Marketing: Greg Worrell • Director, Customer Service Technical Support: Karine Apollon-Mowatt • Associate Director of Customer Service: Pat Drayton

To order more issues or for customer service: 1- 800-SCHOLASTIC

Library of Congress Cataloging-in-Publications Data available ISBN 0-439-39930-0
29 28 27 26   20   Printed in the USA.   First printing X

My 100 Words to Read

Group 1

all	long	slept
drank	man	some
drink	men	take
him	none	took
his	sleep	

Group 2

ask	funny	say
brown	pretty	school
brother	purple	short
child	read	sister
children	said	white

Group 3

both	make	us
but	myself	woman
her	our	women
hers	sang	your
made	sing	

Group 4

cold	Monday	third
first	Saturday	Thursday
Friday	second	Tuesday
keep	small	
kept	Wednesday	
large	Sunday	

Group 5

any	better
every	please
many	thank
few	help
their	town
them	goodbye
best	hello

Group 6

after	then
before	there
here	what
how	when
now	where
open	why
soon	

Group 7

early	quiet
end	spring
fall	story
fell	summer
into	under
more	wide
over	winter

A Smelly Riddle

Word Box

none	take	his
him	men	~~took~~
man	all	

1. Yesterday, he t o o k my picture. Now I will __ __ __ __ his picture.

   1

2. Yesterday, I took __ __ __ dog for a walk. Today, I will walk the

   2

   dog with __ __ __.

   3

3. There is one __ __ __ in the store. There are five __ __ __ on the street.

   4

4. Anna wants __ __ __ of the apples. Carlos wants

   5

   __ __ __ __ of them.

Now look for the numbers under your answers above. Then fill in the matching letters in the blanks below.

What does the owner of a perfume store do?

___ ___ ___ ___ ___ ___ ___ ___ ___ ___ ___ !
2   1   5   5   2   2   3   4   5   5   2

Which Word?

BARBARA GRAY

Directions:
Read the story. Then answer each question with a blue word from the story. We did the first one for you.

Jake was thirsty. "Drink some water," said his mother. Jake drank some water.

Jake was tired. "Go to sleep," said his mother. Jake slept. He took a long nap. When he woke up, he was not thirsty. He was not tired. He was happy.

1 Which blue word begins with **l** and ends with **g**?

   long

2 Which blue word begins with **d** and has an **i** in the middle?

   _____

3 Which blue word ends with a silent **e**?

   _____

4 Which blue word rhymes with **kept**?

   _____

5 Which blue word begins with **s** and rhymes with **deep**?

   _____

6 Which blue word ends with **k** and rhymes with **sank**?

   _____

Shake It Up!

Directions:
To complete the maze, pass only through the **correct** sentences. The correct path will take you through **eight** boxes.

Start

Him makes the best milkshakes.

My father makes milkshakes all the time.

No men makes a better milkshake.

Last week I drank a milkshake every day.

I think his milkshakes are the best.

Last week I drink a milkshake every day.

Today Dad made some milkshakes.

Today Dad didn't make none.

Then he take a short nap.

Then he took a short nap.

While he sleep, I drank a milkshake.

In fact, I drank them all.

In fact, I drinked them all.

While he slept, I drank a milkshake.

I had a stomachache all day!

Finish!

Now try this!
After you've finished, go back and re-read all the boxes you drew a path through. Does your story make sense?

Show and Tell

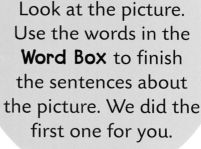

Directions:
Look at the picture. Use the words in the **Word Box** to finish the sentences about the picture. We did the first one for you.

1 It was show-and-tell day at ___school___.

Word Box

purple
brown
white
pretty
funny
short
~~school~~

2 Lilly brought in a fuzzy _____ bear.

3 Jake had a black and _____ zebra.

4 Kim brought a _____ doll in a _____ dress.

5 Joe had a _____ clown that wore _____ pants.

(7)

Directions:
Use the **Word Box** to complete the sentences below. Then write your answers in the correct places in the puzzle. We did the first one for you.

Word Box

brother	read
~~child~~	ask
sister	say
children	said

Across

1 One boy or girl is called a ___child___.

2 Joe and John are twins. Joe is John's _____.

3 Joe _____ hello to Mr. Jones.

4 Tanya loves to _____ books.

Down

5 Joe is Anne's brother. Anne is Joe's _____.

6 Seven _____ came to Tanya's party.

7 Will you _____ Dad for ice cream?

8 Please _____ hello to Mrs. Jones.

¹c h i l d

Sort It Out!

Word Box

~~ask~~	funny	short
brother	said	children
pretty	brown	took
purple	say	sister
read	school	white

Directions:
Put each word from the **Word Box** in the circle where it belongs. We did the first one for you.

People Places Things
(nouns)

_____

_____

_____

Action Words
(verbs)

ask
_____

_____

_____

_____

Describing Words
(adjectives)

_____

_____

_____

_____

_____

9

Directions:
Draw a line from each sentence to the picture it matches. We did the first one for you.

1. This woman is with her little boy.

2. Both women smiled.

3. This bird sang.

4. The children sing songs.

5. The brown and white dog is hers.

Now try this!
Write a sentence using at least two of the blue words on this page.

_____

_____

Find the Word

Word Box

make	us	but
your	myself	
our	~~made~~	

Directions:
Use the words in the **Word Box** to complete the sentences below. Then find each word in the puzzle. We did the first one for you.

1 Lilly _____made_____ a cake for her mother's birthday.

2 I fell down and hurt _____.

3 Jack likes red jelly beans _____ not green ones.

4 Sam will _____ cookies with his friend.

5 What day is _____ birthday?

6 My brother and I went with _____ parents to the park.

7 Our mom took _____ to the zoo.

Hint: Words may go across or down.

d	f	y	o	u	r
m	a	k	e	x	z
a	w	o	b	u	t
d	q	u	l	s	p
e	b	r	m	n	t
m	y	s	e	l	f

Mystery Letter

Directions:
In each set of words, the same letter is missing. Can find the mystery letter in each set? The letters you need are in the **Letter Box.**

Letter Box

i   b   r   n   o

1 he____s
you____
ou____

The mystery letter is ____

2 b____th
w____man
____ur

The mystery letter is ____

5 wome____
sa____g
lo____g

The mystery letter is ____

3 ____ut
____oth
____lack

The mystery letter is ____

Now try this!

To answer the riddle below, fill in the five mystery letters in the order they appear above.

Why did Batman go to the pet store?

4 s____ng
s____ster
wh____te

The mystery letter is ____

To get a ____ ____ ____ ____ ____!
        1   2   3   4   5

Jake's Very Bad Week

Directions:
Read the story. Then fill in the bubble next to the correct ending for each sentence.

I did not have a bad day. I had three bad days! The first one was Monday, when I took my frog to school. He is small, and I kept him in my pocket, but my teacher said I have to keep my frog at home. The second bad day was Wednesday. I forgot we had a spelling test. And my sister put some large ice cubes down my back. They were cold! The third bad day was Saturday. We lost our softball game 37 to 2. I struck out three times. What a week!

1 Jake had a spelling test on
   ○ a. his first bad day.
   ○ b. his second bad day.
   ○ c. his third bad day.

2 Jake's third bad day was
   ○ a. Saturday.
   ○ b. Monday.
   ○ c. Thursday.

3 The opposite of cold is
   ○ a. hot.
   ○ b. freezing.
   ○ c. cool.

4 Another word for small is
   ○ a. little.
   ○ b. large.
   ○ c. silly.

5 The opposite of large is
   ○ a. big.
   ○ b. huge.
   ○ c. small.

6 Jake's teacher said he had to
   ○ a. kept his frog at home.
   ○ b. keeps his frog at home.
   ○ c. keep his frog at home.

Lilly's Busy Month

Directions:
Lilly has a busy month! Use the calendar to answer the questions below. We did the first one for you.

1 Mom's birthday is on the 11th. What day of the week is that? __Sunday__.

2 Lilly plays soccer every _____.

3 Lilly has a dentist's appointment on the _____ Wednesday of the month.
first   second   third

4 The school fair is on the _____ Saturday of the month.
first   second   third

November

Sunday	Monday	Tuesday	Wednesday	Thursday	Friday	Saturday
			1	2	3	
4	5 Play with Janet	6 Soccer 4:00	7	8	9	10 School Fair
11 Mom's birthday	12	13 Soccer 4:00	14	15	16	17
18	19	20 Soccer 4:00	21 Dentist	22 Thanksgiving	23	24
25	26	27 Soccer 4:00	28	29	30	

Recipe for Laughs

Directions:
Don't read this story yet! First, find a partner. One of you will read aloud the words under the blanks at left and write down what the other says. Then put the words in the story and read it out loud.

1._____
    thing (plural)

2._____
    number

3._____
    thing (plural)

4._____
    number

5._____
    color

6._____
    day of week

7._____
    day of week

8._____
    food

9._____
    number

10._____
    number

11._____
    color

Try this yummy recipe for chocolate
_____ . Your friends will love it!
1

• First, put _____ small
    2
_____ in a large bowl.
    3

• Second, add _____
    4
cups of chocolate chips.

• Third, mix until it all turns _____ .
    5

• Bake until _____ , then
    6
keep cold until _____ .
    7

• Serve cold with _____ ice cream
    8
on top.

• Makes _____ servings. It will keep
    9
for _____ weeks. (Once we kept
    10
it longer, but it turned _____ !)
    11

(15)

Picture This!

Directions:
Look at the picture. Then use the words in the **Word Box** to complete the sentences below.

Word Box

Their	Every
any	best
Many	few
better	them

1. _____ butterfly in the picture is yellow.

2. _____ birds in the picture are red.

3. There are a _____ blue birds in the picture.

4. There aren't _____ ants in the picture at all.

5. Tom likes the red birds _____ than the blue ones.

6. Lilly likes the butterflies _____ of all.

7. Tanya likes _____ , too. _____ yellow wings are pretty.

Charlie and Peapod

Directions:
First use the **Word Box** to fill in what these silly dogs say to each other. Then complete Charlie's last sentence.

Word Box

Goodbye   hello   please   Thank   help   town

---

1 Hi, Peapod! May I
___ ___ ___ ___ ___ ___
                1
ask you a question?

2 Why, ___ ___ ___ ___ ___ ,
Charlie! Please do!   **2**

3 How do I get to
___ ___ ___ ___ , Peapod?

4 I am happy to ___ ___ ___ ___ .
Just cross the street.

5 ___ ___ ___ ___ ___ ___ you, Peapod.
___ ___ ___ ___ ___ ___ !
   3   **4**   **5**

6 You're welcome, Charlie. By the way, why are you going to town?

7 I need a raincoat, Peapod. I don't want to be a
___ ___ ___ ___ ___   ___ ___ ___ ___ ___ !
  1 **2** **3** **3** **5**   **4** **2** **3** **3** **5**

(17)

BARBARA GRAY

A-maze-ing Apples

Start

Hello! May I please buy some apples?
1

Them apples look tasty.

We buy apples here every year.

Apples pleases me.
2

He help me reach the apples.

The ripe apples are over their.

I won't buy any green apples.

Few apples taste as good as these.

Thanks you for the apples.
6

Green apples are best than red apples.

I like red apples better than green.
4

Many apples is ripe.
3

Thanks for the apples. Goodbye!

Many apples are ripe.
5

Finish

Now try this! To answer the riddle, look for the numbers under some of the letters inside the maze. Then fill in the matching letters below.

What kind of apple isn't an apple?

__ __ __ __ __ __ __ __ __ __!
2 1 5 4 3 2 1 1 6 3

Which Word?

Directions:
Read the story. Then answer each question with a blue word from the story. We did the first one for you.

My little brother Jack loves school so much that one day he was the first one there! "May I come in now and get to work?" he asked his teacher.

"But Jack, school is not open yet," she said. "You are here before all the other kids. Soon the other children will be here. After that, it will be time for school to start. Then we will all get to work!" The next day, the school was closed when Jack got there. Was he the first one there? No, he was the only one there. It was Saturday!

1. Which blue word sounds the same as the word **hear** and means **in this place**?

   here

2. Which blue word means the opposite of **closed**?

   _____

3. Which blue word sounds the same as **their** and means **in that place**?

   _____

4. Which blue word means **at this time** and rhymes with **cow**?

   _____

5. Which two blue words are opposites? (**Hint:** One starts with **a** and the other starts with **b**.)

   _____

   _____

6. Which blue word starts with **t** and rhymes with **when**?

   _____

What's the Question?

Directions:
Use the words in the **Word Box** to write the question that each sentence answers. We did the first one for you.

Word Box

who   ~~when~~   why

what   where   how

---

1 **Answer:** The soccer game is after school on Monday.

Question: When is the soccer game ?

2 **Answer:** That is my friend Sam.

Question:_____
_____?

3 **Answer:** My last name is Brown.

Question:_____
_____?

4 **Answer:** School closed because it snowed.

Question:_____
_____?

5 **Answer:** The books are here.

Question:_____
_____?

6 **Answer:** The dog reached the cookies by jumping on the table.

Question:_____
_____?

Sort It Out!

Word Box

after	~~sister~~	now	there
children	before	school	us
here	men	soon	

Who?
(people words)
sister
_____

_____

_____

_____

Where?
(place words)
_____

_____

_____

When?
(time words)
_____

_____

_____

_____

The Terrible Tooth Fairy

Directions:
This memo to the Queen Tooth Fairy is missing some words! Find them in the **Word Box** and write them in the correct spaces.

Word Box

wide	into	end
quiet	over	early
more	story	fell

To: Queen Tooth Fairy
From: Complaint Department

We have had many complaints about Tooth Fairy Number 324, also known as Doris. Last Saturday she got to work too _____ , before the boy was asleep. When she flew_____ the top of his head, he jumped out of bed and chased her with a can of bug spray.

And that's not the _____ of the _____. She also broke Tooth Fairy Rule #1: Be _____! Last week, she took a nap in a kid's doll house and _____ off the little bed. The girl woke up and started to cry. When Doris flew away, she left the doll house door _____ open.

We cannot let Doris get _____ any _____ trouble. Please find her a new job. I hear the Easter Bunny needs help this year. Thank you.

The Four Seasons

Directions:
Write the name of each season where it belongs in the puzzle below. For each one, we've given you a word and a picture as clues.

Word Box

summer   spring
winter   fall

1
l
e
a
v
e
s

2
s n o w

3
r o b i n s

4
g r a s s

Now try this!

The four seasons have their letters all mixed up! Can you unscramble them?

lafl _____

gripns _____

etnriw _____

rmesum _____

True or False?

Directions: To complete the maze, pass only through the boxes containing **true** statements. The correct path takes you through **seven** boxes.

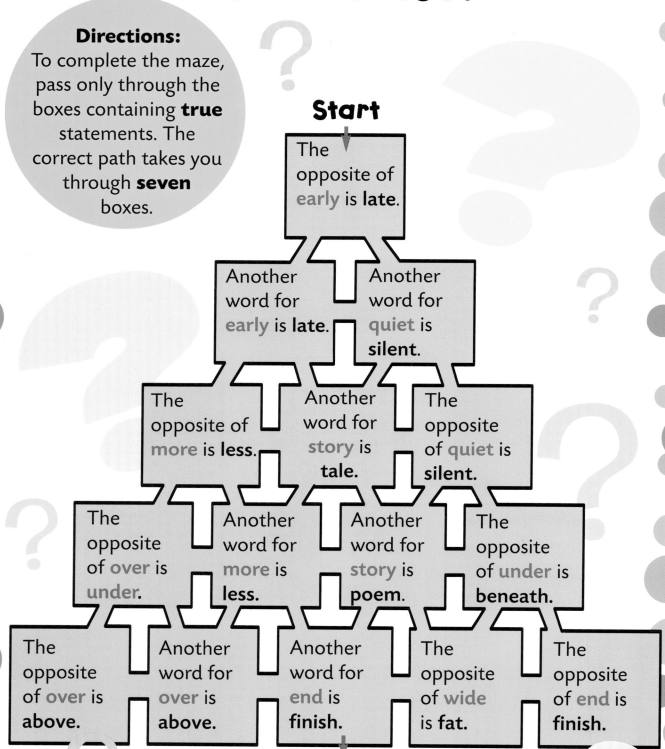

Start

The opposite of **early** is **late**.

Another word for **early** is **late**.

Another word for **quiet** is **silent**.

The opposite of **more** is **less**.

Another word for **story** is **tale**.

The opposite of **quiet** is **silent**.

The opposite of **over** is **under**.

Another word for **more** is **less**.

Another word for **story** is **poem**.

The opposite of **under** is **beneath**.

The opposite of **over** is **above**.

Another word for **over** is **above**.

Another word for **end** is **finish**.

The opposite of **wide** is **fat**.

The opposite of **end** is **finish**.

Finish!

better	fell	please
cold	funny	purple
drank	help	read
every	our	said

Name That Word!

Name That Word!

Name That Word!

Name That Word!

Name That Word!

Name That Word!

Name That Word!

Name That Word!

Name That Word!

Name That Word!

Name That Word!

Name That Word!

slept	them	who
spring	Wednesday	winter
some	third	wide
thank	what	women

Word Cards for Name That Word! game. See page 29.

Name
That
Word!

Name
That
Word!

Name
That
Word!

Name
That
Word!

Name
That
Word!

Name
That
Word!

Name
That
Word!

Name
That
Word!

Name
That
Word!

Name
That
Word!

Name
That
Word!

Name
That
Word!

Name That Word! Board Game

What You Need to Play
- The game board on pages 30–31 of this book
- Word Cards (cut from pages 25–28 of this book)
- Two players
- A game piece for each player (like a coin or a button)
- One die

How to Play
- Place all the Word Cards facedown in a pile.
- Roll the die. Move your piece the number of dots on the die.
- If you land on a pink circle, say a word that rhymes with the word in the circle.
- If you land on "Pick a Card," your partner picks a Word Card and reads the word on the card out loud. You have to spell it. If you spell the word correctly, move ahead one space. After you follow the directions on that space, it is your partner's turn.
- If you land on any other circle, follow the directions.
- The first person to reach *Finish* wins!

Now Try This!
You can use your Word Cards without the game board to play other games, like Memory:
- Combine 12 of your cards with the same 12 of a friend's cards. (Use either all of your green cards or all of your orange cards.) Mix them up.
- Spread all the cards facedown. The cards should not overlap.
- Pick a card and turn it over. Now pick another card and turn it over. If the two words match, take both cards and keep them. Go again until you turn over two cards that do not match.
- The other player does the same.
- The game is over when there are no cards left. The player with the most cards wins!

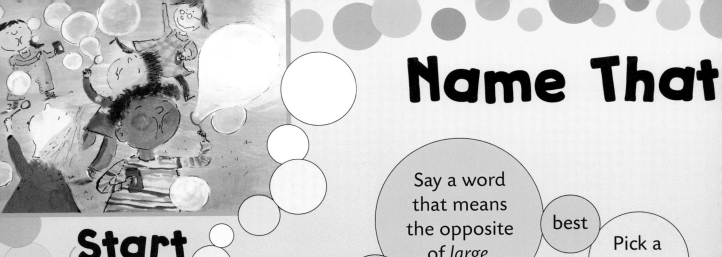

Name That

Start

all

Pick a card.

Say the name of the day of the week that comes after Saturday.

drink

Go ahead one space.

more

Spell the word that sounds the same as *hear* but means "at this place."

Pick a card.

soon

Say a word that means the opposite of *large*.

Pick a card.

Say a word that means the opposite of *long*.

now

Go back one space.

make

Spell a word that sounds the same as *their* but means "in that place."

best

Pick a card.

Say the word that rhymes with *ring* and means what one might do to a song.

man

Pick a card.

Say a word that means the opposite of *quiet*.

school

Go ahead o space

ord!

Say a word for the season that comes after summer.

took

town

Say the question word that asks about time.

Say a word that means the opposite of *after*.

Say the word at rhymes with *ory* and means a tale.

Go back one space.

Pick a card.

say

Say the word that rhymes with *wild* and means a young person.

Say a word that means the opposite of *early*.

Pick a card.

who

Pick a card.

Say the word that rhymes with *task* and means "to say a question."

white

Pick a card.

Say a word that means the same as *small*.

where

Say the word that starts with *f* and means "not very many."

why

Pick a card.

end

Say a word that means the opposite of *under*.

ay the word rhymes with *eep* and tells what a tired erson does.

Finish!

Notes